D1558138

lousy explorers

lousy explorers

LAISHA ROSNAU

NIGHTWOOD EDITIONS

Nightwood Editions
Box 1779
Gibsons, BC Canada V0N 1V0

The book has been produced on 100% post-consumer recycled, ancient-forest-free paper, processed chlorine -free and printed with vegetable-based dyes.

Design by Michelle Winegar

Nightwood Editions acknowledges financial support of its publishing program from the Canada Council for the Arts and the Book Publishing Industry Development Program (BPIDP), and from the British Columbia Arts Council.

Canada Council Conseil des Arts
for the Arts du Canada

LIBRARY AND ARCHIVES CANADA CATALOGUING IN PUBLICATION

Rosnau, Laisha, 1972-
    Lousy explorers / Laisha Rosnau.

Poems.
ISBN 978-0-88971-230-0

    I. Title.

PS8585.O8336 L68 2009   C811'.6   C2009-901310-X

For Aaron, my fellow explorer
of the lousy, the sublime, and everything in between

But the dark pines of your mind dip deeper
And you are sinking, sinking, sleeper
In an elementary world;
There is something down there and you want it told.

–Gwendolyn MacEwen
"Dark Pines Under Water"

contents

BUSHING SUBURBIA

She inflates the yard
with rubber boats, leaves them
full to fold grass, make gold
patterns on the lawn.

Diapers clipped to the line
like cut-out hearts or the skin
of small mammals, flying
squirrels perhaps, hung to clean.

The birch is felled, messages
to its roots cut off but it still sends
runners, erupts the lawn.
She mows the tiny trees,

knows there is something happening
under there, forests unplanted,
the hidden lightning of fine shoots
branching, taking hold.

LOOK AT US: 1972

I had my doubts, a city full of people
who spoke foreign languages, politics stable
as a sagging dock taking on water,
my marriage similar in ways,
different in most others.

I sent a few things flying in the kitchen,
hid symptoms so well that not even I knew I had them.
For a few weeks, I thought I was hung-over,
later told my daughter that obviously
a little wine with dinner had hurt no one.

I wore my hair dyed golden to my head, a cap.
Maternity clothes were more fun back then—
leotards topped with triangles of fabric,
colours going off, all jaunty and paisley
like eddied glee, spiked laughter.

I met some great women. Here, look at us:
my cat-rimmed glasses and love of orange,
her rope of waist-length hair and, for that one,
every garment had chimes or tassels. Look at
our three bellies, those skin-bound moons.

Weekends, we lamented the drugs dropped
and smoked in the last decade, missed
them a bit, while someone's husband
lit the hibachi and the guys got fired up
about hockey scores and changing weather.

Nothing was worse than then,
nothing was better. I had my moods.

WEEKEND VISITING RIGHTS

The wind, a weight in lungs, drops
through branches, snatches needles,
and presses her back to her mother's house.
From an upstairs window, light is released
onto the lawn, cross-marked by panes.
Her mother's calls come from inside—*Oh,
oh, oh!*—and the night forest, with its air
like steam engines through trees,
smell of spruce and loam, is much less
than the sound of the two of them,
ragged and rejoicing, the final *Oh God!*
large enough to contain a beginning
and an end, she's not yet sure which it will be,
if the man will stay. Morning might tell.

Over breakfast, she will say to them:
*I was out past dark until I couldn't see
the pages of my book.* She probably won't
mention that sleep is tricky in this house.
What they say will let her know
whether she should stay or call her father,
go back to the city. The leather seats
of his new car still hold their smell for her.

CENTURY 21

Our mother was in real estate, entered
the business when business was almost flat,
a quaver of air along the prairie at forty below.

What a warm figure she cut in brown and gold:
knee-high boots the colour of dark chocolate,
so snug her calves looked dipped, fondued—

and tortoise-shell glasses, the circumference
of each lens as big as the two baby turtles
we kept in a tank in the basement.

It wasn't all about location, our mother
explained at the dinner table; sometimes
it was as simple as how things looked.

Our own school photos were framed,
ready by the door in case our mother
needed to add something to a stranger's house—

our gleaming bowl cuts, smiles open
to potential buyers, our missing teeth
only a sign of what was to come.

SUBTLE MUTATIONS

You abandon the car and walk
into a Roman afternoon.
You know how to kill your father,
he knows how to kill you.

–Mary di Michele, "How to Kill Your Father"

You never lived inside his body—no shared blood or mucous,
no rip in him where you emerged. You are linked instead
by code stamped with dominance, subtle mutations.
His features, visible in yours at birth, take over later:
Roman nose, peaked lips. You share an aggravation
with objects that cannot be fixed by thought alone.

Later, you figure out how to kill parts of each other
slowly with blows finer and more forceful
than slammed doors or thrown crockery. It is language
that does it. One winter afternoon, you watch light
off snow enter the room, spark around his shoulders
as they shake, sobs avalanching off. You had lobbed
those three words, the hot brand of *hate* searing the middle.

Your brother skis into a tree; branches drop their weight
over his eyes, goggled and unconscious—that is what it takes
from him to make your father cry. With you, it was words,
and just that once. Years later, you will decide to abandon
your car at the side of the highway, the hatchback not worth it.
You are relieved that neither you nor your dad is very handy.
You were once able to kill each other. Now you'd rather leave
what's broken to the ditch, know you can always walk home.

SOMETHING ABOUT PARADES IS ALWAYS A LITTLE SAD

The cowgirl from the Kispiox has been taken
into town in her boyfriend's pickup. They drive
for more than an hour just to get to a 7-Eleven.
Once there, he tells her to wait and she sits
on the bench seat, snaps gum.
When the door opens she's not surprised to see
someone else. This man takes her to Vancouver,
sells her body on the street, keeps the proceeds.
I meet her later, discuss line breaks, sharp images,
the sound of teenage boys caterwauling
on crystal meth in the park behind my back fence.
I recognize one, weeks later, when he turns up dead
in the newspaper. His father mistook crashing
around the bush for a lost moose and shot, his child
gone but here longer than those of three friends
whose four babies live for less than a day combined,
the hours barely bruised by their light breath.

✦

I pump my heart until it beats like a marjorette's drum
—'til it twirls sticks with quick wrists, wears cute ankle socks—
and I send it out into the world. It goes a-soaring,
is borne skyward. Up and up it rides, past forests
infested with beetles, flooding river deltas, bogs on fire.
It takes on clouds, charms them with its booming
song and dance until my heart is exhausted,
falls to earth, a parade trailing behind it in paper flowers.
Princesses wave—all afloat—candy rains
from open palms and hits you in the chest, the clown
on the tricycle brings up the rear,
and we all hold parts of ourselves a little closer.

CONFLUENCE

Train tracks lace cut banks, expose their clay underbellies,
certain of themselves even as they wear away.
Makeshift porches jut out of the front end of trailers.
We walk the mudflats, the sound of banjos in our mouths.
Is that cottonwood fluff caught in your beard?

This place a contradiction, a clouded seam
where two currents meet, the stitching visible
—rail cars crash into each other, the mill plumes,
pulping the air, a red-tailed hawk lifts off
a spruce tree, flies toward the prison.

We walk under bridges, toe the river's frayed edge
then slip in, shoes on and clothed, float toward the confluence.
We let go of each other's hands, choose alternate routes
around islands of silt, meet where it is shallow,
knees banging against rocks until

the colour of water warns it is time to pull out:
around the bend, the larger river will take over.
Twinned and eager, it cuts corners and draws them
down, muddy skirts fanning out behind. On shore
we meet, dripping, point out broken glass in the reeds,
the slow light it catches, slivers of sky in the bank.

ENGLISH MAJORS

You had me quaking with a smile, knock-kneed
and fingering my pockets for a smoke.
Skin brown from living on a beach, bungee
cord as belt, I lit up before I spoke,
and we shared a match in long-john weather.
Neither of us said it was too early
for frost but tongued the words, wondered whether
it mattered at all. So young and wary
already of the things we might say to
each other—semantics and post-modern
paradigms fucking up our soft minds. You
remarked *Nice belt*, and I exhaled and turned
away from the smoke then offered my hook:
Easy access, my face an open book.

FIRST FALL

Tangled under the pallid glow of stars
on the ceiling of your small apartment,
we shared a single bed, everything ours—
dirty sheets and clean drugs, demands for rent,
UI cheques, sweeter than fruit to us then.
Pot-warmed afternoons pinned us to park grass,
kites against sky snapped, bold as the nights when
we soaked in stage lights, beamed until they passed.
It was time we had to kill, weeks idling
until the day you found me in the spill
of light from the fridge, my arms cradling
an empty milk carton. You held me 'til
the shaking stopped, your love my only coup
that fall, stars radiant without a moon.

RESTRAINT

That night on the Alaska Highway, it
was May. I still smelled of sticky fruit, Thai
markets, months spent away. When the snow hit
your fever started and was followed by
reluctance when I suggested we stop,
sleep in a motel instead of a tent.
Hands clutched around mugs in the coffee shop,
we didn't talk, I wondered what it meant
to have borne my restraint through each country
without you. I wore glasses, skin covered,
coiled my hair so tight no curl twisted free,
got smaller in each new mirror, discovered
how to go unseen. There was no heat when
I returned, my mind spored with other men.

PROOF

Tell me about the beautiful
numbers, their perfection
primed, how everything

adds up, brilliantly if not simply.
I have seen what you call proof
and know that it is pages

as I can understand pages,
one after the other and so on
and so on, yours marked

not with the words I am
used to shaking loose until
they become sound, set

to paper. Your pages are
a cacophony of symbols,
each resonating off the others

and for all the discord—trembling
falsettos, sharp notes on the way—
when you finally reach the end

they come to a place of precision,
pages reverberating on one brilliant
chord. Though, not really:

the numbers don't add up
as they should, leave a black
hole between the big and small,

theories circling the lip
until they are swallowed,
become nothing.

Each point is also a wave
containing all possibilities;
our universe a girl in a bar,

night spread out before her,
a row of glittering drinks,
how much and who unknown.

I don't want that. I want you
to prove there is only one answer
and the answer is yes.

PART OPEN

We live in a rental house
surrounded by aspens,
grass brown both summer
and winter. We're thankful
for blankets of snow,
what they hide.

We sleep in the hottest corner
of the house, covers folded
around our ankles, curtains
drawn from June to August.
Later we will part them,
uncover cold blue light.

We pretend we are alone,
the two of us, season to season,
love each other loudly,
ignore the vents and the people
downstairs, their coughs
white noise.

We keep our childhood
in the freezer. Late at night
we go to the kitchen, open light
into the room then close the door,
pass a spoon back and forth
in the dark, tongues melting.

HABITAT

Her mother is from a place called Hope,
gets work after graduation in a abattoir,
light pocked with chicken feathers,
the tickle and prick a memory on skin
long after the job is done.
Savings shed along the Trans-Canada,
she arrives in Montreal, welcomed
with a song—*Hey friend, Say friend!*
—the world smiles with her. She stands
in front a hive of stacked concrete
cubes that someone has called an ideal home
on an island of pavilions ballooning
out of the Saint Lawrence.
*See how each tilts toward the sun
at a slightly different incline*, the man
beside her says, and she angles
her eyes upward, looks past him
and says she thinks it ugly, their first disagreement,
deflected when he asks her where she's from
and they decide to pull the country out
between them, wait for something to give.

CRISIS

She lives in a thin stone house on a short block
between the hardware store and the church,
convent crowning the street before it slips
into Lac Saint-Louis. She and the nuns both
wear garments that conceal, theirs the slim turn
of ankle, twist of waist, hers the swell
of stretched mid-section, the thudding
inside her, a boat against the shore.
She seeks trees, crawls into the shade
they flounce over grass.

In autumn, two men are kidnapped.
After they are found dead, one locked
in the trunk of a car at the airport,
my mother dreams of them banging
at her from the inside out, heavy fists
on metal. She wakes with the taste
of iron on her tongue, knows we will
be two. In one moment, her pregnancy
is twinned, the television casting light
on the room as the War Measures Act
is invoked, relief and defiance
flush on the Prime Minister's face.

Our mother decides we should move
to the other side of the country,
tells our father when he gets home,
then they wait out the winter.
We arrive early, a few weeks
before the moving trucks.
Wet and stained with our cramped
passage, our hands unfurl
and mouths gape when held under
the lamp, eyes closed in the light.

CARELESS GEOGRAPHY

For months, the back of the car
became a bed, boxes piled,
topped with blankets and books,
our heads flung back, faces tipped
open, bowled over by sky.

The contents of our former house
ranged across the top of the continent
without us, while we drove south,
whimsied over magnolias,
Mickey Mouse, hoodoos.

Every day, Dolly Parton's voice
sweet clover and Johnny Cash's
a train coming down the line
as we listened for the clang of bells,
crossed over a country of tracks.

Montana came in December. Mom drove
across the northern border, gave in
to wheels coaxed on by black ice.
We three-sixtied three times. My brother and I,
the glee club in the back, called for more.

When we stopped, the horizon
was flat, marked by the triangular roofs
of our parents' childhood homes.
Blue sky stamped against snow, white paint
chipping from walls. We would stay until spring.

Until then, cows clouded mornings
with their damp noses. We criss-crossed
patterns into the frozen pond, skated
our own careless geography,
stopped only when our cheeks hurt.

EARLY GIRLS GET WORN

Your mother told you, get your head
out of the clouds, but the whirr of air
filled your ears, made it impossible to hear.
Mouths open and close, tongues
the colour of bruises, thick as brambles.

Lick your finger—mouth popping
around the tip—then prick the needle
into those first layers, pin your skin
to the moment, ask yourself:
if this is a stitch in time, what has been saved?

If early birds get the worm, then—
wait, what about that one about the cow
and the milk? You want to wake up
with the sun, follow animals to pasture,
lie there until you're too hot to move.

IF THUNDER IS ANYTHING

Clouds refuse to give over the lake
so we swim under the threat of lightning
Crescents of dirt under fingernails
seem permanent, as if I'd been mining
a deep vein of mineral. If you must

compare my body to something
make it a comma—albeit with more
curves than that coy eyelash—
a symbol that says: there is this
and wait, there is also this.

I have to learn to forgive my skin
as neither perfect, nor proof of me
ending, the world beginning. It keeps
letting everything in: water, currents
of air, the cold, good things as well—you.

If thunder is anything, it is your face lit.
It is what we do to each other, again and again,
no apologies, the thump-thump
of blood in our ears, your heart
big as a bear breathing at the door of the tent.

COOLING-OFF PERIOD

Something in the car
clicks when it cools,
stones spun out from road,
underwheel to underbelly,

an erratic tick, uneven countdown,
like the decay of accelerated particles
recorded with the spastic tock
of machinery, sprays of light congealed.

Time is married to change
but I don't budge, my mood
a pie on the counter, heat rising
off the surface. I wield the road

like a pastry knife, hope the slice
of highway will release some steam.
Bruised fruit when bitten sours
the tongue with the taste of damage

but even it can be preserved,
sweetness added and sealed
into jars and crusts. The question is:
what to save, what to compost.

I would hardly call it cool, my mind
after the drive, but the pie is the perfect
temperature when I return.
He hands me a piece, still warm.

WINTER DRIVING, THIRD TRIMESTER

Trees cage a dull white sky, bare ribs
of branches still, no diaphragm of wind
to fill them. Breath snagged in my chest,

torn and then winched upward
along vertebrae until it catches on my skull,
reverberates then settles behind my eyes.

A squall of snow presses against the windows,
wipes trees from the roadside, a single lane
of hazard lights flares ahead. Their wake settles

before I pass in the wrong lane, flip the tail
of the car in a slight spin then slide into gravel
and salt-eased grooves. The fleet creeps less

from caution than reverence, enters the cemetery,
a chain of vehicles made colourless
by weather. I follow the frozen river

until I leave it for a plateau, trees hunched
in white, five types of house plan repeated,
my driveway lined up with the rest, collecting snow.

The sound of shovels against concrete shunts
up the street. I open the front door and the baby kicks,
tiny foot pushing through heat until my bones move.

THOSE DREAMS OF TEETH

Inside us, cells divide, swell, skim off
(bubbles on the surface of milk)
Outside, the face becomes a map,
the body begins to relax, express itself
more loosely, while the mind tightens

(lips wrapped around a finger, peach
around a pit, a contraction) clings
to past fancies.

How lucky the sky is to never know
the meaning of *horizon*, to simply take
what it is given, show us with colour,
cover of clouds, spray of stars,
how things are—how high,
how light, dark, empty, how—

> one word repeated becomes
> the sound of the loss of meaning.

It is impossible to speak
with your mouth flung open.
Jaw wide on its hinges,
sounds will hum in the throat
but can't press against the tongue.

Those dreams of teeth you have?
They let you know how you feel
about fences—where the openings are,
what can be hauled out, replaced (how it feels
to tongue the soft gaps left behind).

Your body grows around the certainty
of another at its centre—a second
heartbeat submerged, topography
of spectred limbs against skin.

You are forced open by a crown,
a toothless cry, all former fence-posts
pulled up, ground gaping.
You can walk for miles.

I'VE GOT YOU: AUGUST 1981

1.

Temperature mounted until it became a body
of heat, crush of weight holding us down.
Weather reports looped—*it is getting hotter
and hotter*—and news became a tally
of missing children, ten in less than a year.
They would be found hoarding the cold,
clutching it in ditches, ravines, groves of trees
so thick they held perpetual dusk by day,
wholescale darkness by night.

2.

We were not allowed outside alone, discovered
it was finesse, not force, that was needed
to play ping-pong properly, squeezed
the plastic balls instead, their *pop!* so satisfying.
Wanting something cooler on our palms,
we helped each other reach the exposed
pipes, underbelly of the hotel, and swung
until we were swatted off by staff,
ordered back to our room.

3.

Our mother on the bed, face shrouded
with a wet cloth folded up
off her mouth. Our father stood,
Scotch in hand, staring down
the television. *Sick bastard*, he said.
When our mother got up and passed by
the screen flickered, smeared the fabric
of her slip. *They caught him*,
she told us, *we'll all feel better now.*

4.

Yorkshire pudding steamed when opened
so easily, the roast beef caught in the teeth
of our knives, not as rare as we wanted.
Indulged, we were allowed any kind of drink,
ordered Shirley Temple and Roy Rogers
to the table, frosted glasses, submerged
maraschinos bleeding bright. The Big Band
faltered through Air Supply then returned
to Sinatra, doors open, sounds crooned across the pool:

> *I've got you under my skin*, laughter, splintering
> glass when the drink slipped from my hand,
> calves cool before the liquid dried
> to the kind of sticky that comes with sweet.

THE TASTE OF IRON

When she asked, *Where are we going?*
truck pointed in the wrong direction,
headed for the hills,
burned grass and black trees,
she didn't expect a straight answer.

Didn't expect the arm cocked,
vice-gripped around her neck,
rush of blood and the hot metal
of his button fly on her cheek, hair twisted
into her mouth, the taste of iron.

She didn't know that her body
could buck like that, lie in wait
then crack, jagged and white hot,
kick open the door to fresh air,
crickets' legs caught on night, rubbing.

The distance into town was too long.
A cougar reported on the news, sly
and muscled, lurked with night vision,
nothing but red thoughts.
She got back in the truck, knowing

the cat's eyes would only be a flash
in the headlights. She knew she could
keep her wrist draped over the handle, wait
for flat roads and soft ditches. She knew
the right way to roll into a fall, yield to it.

CREEK BED

End of summer, edge of the yard smudged
under hands and knees, back rubbing against
cedar hedge, the boy is intent on the bush,
the way it clings to cut-bank, sheds itself
into the ravine.

On the side of the house a window slices
a square of light above the woman, a shadow
on the wall below. A man pulls away,
fist of her hair in his hand, laughs
a quick punch of air that hits the boy.

He hears his father, sees his neighbour,
hair spread like a stain. Belly to ground,
he drags himself toward the lip of the cut-bank,
listens to blood bang in his ears, shrill
of voices from an open door—

then nothing but the creek, once high
now chafed against exposed rocks,
running until it runs dry as his mouth,
tongue heavy, stuck.

SPRING CLEANING

Your face gives me a nosebleed, he said,
meant as a compliment, something
about being high. He worried
when she missed her monthly. *No,
it's not that*, she said.
She'd picked up a parasite
while travelling and it was still curled
within her, eating through enough fat
that she no longer bled.

Perhaps their bodies sensed
the bear, cannily kept them inside
while the yearling tore up the dog,
streaked the river red.
She watched the water, twisted
with swollen wood, wondered
where she would end up
if she ran off with the spring.

After they found the dog dead,
he could still hear it at night,
coil of wind in its chain,
tracks scratched around its post.
She watched him sleep, slapped
at the sound of mosquitoes,
heard the river shuffling around rocks,
knew the water had gone down.

That winter, she would give up sugar,
meat, dairy, even beer, will her body
to self-insulate. He'd forego nothing
then huge chunks of him would give,
only to form a trap, like ice crammed
in the river until spring break-up tore it away.
By then she would already be gone, a stain
left on the sheets, cupboards stripped
of feminine products, body purged.

WE WOULD LIKE SOMETHING FOR DESSERT...

1.

But only something good. Give us a sundae, please,
top it with a cherry. Let go the rest of the week,
Saturday on one side with her skirt flipped up,
Monday on the other, palm open for spare change
outside the liquor store. We would like someone,
a paper-skinned schoolmarm, perhaps, to call
out each day of the week—*Wednesday, you take gym class
too seriously; Friday, you are like old candy, sucked
and then put back in the bowl*—and send them
out on garbage duty. We need someone like that
around here, someone to order our days, let us know
when it's time for the sweetness that follows.

2.

The girls are always out, bare legs so thin they are like pins,
holding down the corners of streets, pricked into Main
and Terminal down there, Queensway and Second here,
stretching our province thin, holding it in place
until something rips, curls away from the edge.
The Fraser cuts cold air through town, the stench of mills
rides piggyback, everything that can fall in
catches a ride south. Bodies of ice dissolve the whole way,
nothing but murk by the time they reach the ocean.
Up here, the ladies are lined up with the men outside
St. Vincent de Paul, waiting for the days of the week to file in
as they should, waiting for something good at the end.

THE DRIVE HOME

At eighteen you leave that place,
foam mattress tied with rope, box of books,
friend with a jeep: all out of the valley by noon.
Can you forget the smell of apples,
pollen clinging to lake?

In the city, you give your body up
for a few years in the name
of weightlessness. Your mind
mushrooms like spores, jellied and bulbous,
toxic clouds in a distant desert.

The body of a friend gives up on its own ghost
while yours feigns sleep like dead weight.
When your mind begins to tear strips
off illusion until there is only exposed bone,
it's time to leave, to drive home.

Afterward, you will remember bus rides
on acid, a city streaked with light
as you tried to read Tolstoy—
horses in snow, empty ballrooms
and the heavy sound of trains on tracks.

Your mom knows the city can age you
twenty years in two: bruises under the skin
that bloom unseen, smell of dust and metal.
She suggests therapy. On drives there
and back together, the lake switches sides,
lets you know whether you're coming or going.

BACHELOR SUITE

Here there are no true birds, only gulls that dive for things
that fell to the roofs below in the dark. Evenings, the crows
fly east, carry the last light as they smudge the sky.

By nightfall my room is frayed by voices—you lament birds
untethered from cut trees, your mind spooling around itself, my reply
threadbare. Thoughts turn inward, a cat nesting in the laundry.

Days, the space composes itself in parts, a small tapestry of functions
—bed folded into a couch, desk, windows that let the sun
toy with my things before night sews it all back together.

The raised bathroom in the middle—the tub's balled claws
holding it in place—sutures the part of the room that means *eat*
to the part that means *get dressed, write, fight, make love.*

There is space enough for one, really. A room written for solo
performances backed by sirens and car horns. Another can join in, granted
the right tone and range, but only when voices stop can night start.

Birds pick at sleep's stitching, gather threads in their beaks to line nests.
We wake to nothing but sun in the room, hatchlings
hitting the windows, confusing us with sky.

HE WAS THE NUMBER 14

He was the Number 14, a bus ride
down Hastings one way, strung
with blinking lights and sparks
of trolleys unhooked, headed
to Arbutus, the salt lick of ocean,
tongues swollen to lap up the whole thing.

He was a drum kit under the full skirt
of a tree, rain trenched around it.
Kicked out of a cab near Lost Lagoon,
he was a cedar thick enough
to keep the drum's skin dry and tight,
a snared lullaby before sleep.

He was chain-links around the marina,
winches loosed by wind, rigging
played against spar and mast like chimes
frothed into a frenzy. He was the mainstay
snapped and boom slammed into the dock,
light splintered on black water.

He was the underside of Cambie St. Bridge,
algae barnacled lace on pilings, twisted
salal of fire growing out of a barrel, boys
playing basketball, steady ring of rubber
against pavement echoed off False Creek,
a watered-down version of tides.

He was a billboard crowning a brick building
on Main and Broadway, images of thirst
unsated on the outside, inside a keyhole
in a metal door, wooden staircase, space
between signs. He was a murmur of rock doves,
lights weaving mountains into a nest.

BUG SEASON ON BIG THING MOUNTAIN

Halfway up, I realize I'm missing
bug spray, bed down in a structure
partially built by karma-plagued Yukoners
who aspired towards Tibet, left this place
unfinished, half-holy. I unroll a sleeping bag
on what there is of a floor.

I wonder if it was bugs that drove Buddhists
from this place. Imagine, disciples
descending the mountain, minds hot fireweed,
desires sharp—a cessation of the building
of this temple rather than of thought.
The word *stop* becomes emotion, fettered

to the body. I can't slide under the smooth shell
of sleep, though my eyes are nearly swollen shut
with blood drawn from my lids to feed the eggs
of insects. I picture each mosquito
robed, her hum a high-pitched chant,
as they take from me offerings,

like oranges and poppies at the feet of statues,
except my blood carries the desire for death
to all insects, supplications sent
echoing in the hollow temple of sleep.

SMALL KINGDOM

Saturday morning, he is there,
a small king in a Toronto market.

Double espresso and tobacco,
rolled into leaf-thin paper.

Morning repeats its refrain in light—
silvered off the bells of bikes,

trembling coins the trees toss
from branch to branch.

And now he is here—sun ricochets
off the surface of the truck,

the front-ends of animals
swallowed by bush.

He pulls over, counts the sound
of birds, their calls plump with spring.

She can see him, here and there, no binaries
under clothes, skin a simple unifier.

Next winter, he'll turn to her
in the bed, their small kingdom.

In their dens, bears will roll
inward around dreams of fruit.

SISTER LIFE

Life haunted by its more beautiful sister life—
Always, always…

—Charles Simic, "Promises of Leniency and Forgiveness"

Afternoons in that diner on Main Street,
people lined up at the bus stop in the rain
on the other side of the window while I ordered
salad then ate all his leftover fries.
I lived in the sky—light from three directions,
a view of bridges and high rises full of people
I would never meet. I was so small up there,
mountains ringing my vision, dazzled
when the right song played, the wood floors
were clean and rainbows arced over cranes.

Evenings, husbands and boyfriends
of other women cocked grins, passed wine, grazed
my wrists and I was giddy with thoughts
of cheese platters, hotel rooms
I'd stay in late or leave early to catch cabs
in last night's clothes, tissue stuck to the heel of my shoe.
People went to work, paper cups in hand,
steam clinging to them like sleep.
Rain streaked the windows, gulls shrieked
over dead things on the roof below.
What beautiful sister life was elsewhere,
in a frost-etched city or held in the hand of a man
who didn't have my phone number?

I will never be an architect in Montreal
but I can mourn the trappings—a loft
converted from something industrial or something rural,
art hung high on the walls, for the children
a nanny, more likely Slavic than Asian.
Photo crews would bear witness to a well-appointed
Bohemian lifestyle—ladder of reclaimed wood
rolling along the shelves in the library, jazz filtered
through unseen speakers, blown glass pitchers
of fruit-laced sangria catching light like rubies.

Here we are, you and I and a bi-level bungalow
in a town built on the milled trees of a forest
eaten by bugs that burrow into wood,
leave behind decay the colour of twilight.
I tap keys, listen for studs and supports,
soft spots and signs of rot. Ordinary sounds
surprise me, a dog barking, the creak
then slam of mail dropped in the box.
My sister life sends word from other places.
I steam off stamps and save them.

MOVING DAY

We carry things that have outlived their first owners—
my grandparent's teapot, a toaster you were given
for helping an old lady move one winter in Toronto,
chrome clouding in the cold when you walked home.

In my state, I should not do any heavy lifting,
the heft and twist of boxes not recommended.
I am carrying enough already, a second heartbeat,
someone who owns nothing yet but the centre of me.

It is the small things that conceal their mass—a box
of polished rocks, photographs packed tight—
and pain breaks my movement, empties my hands,
leaves me staring out the window above the sink until

some forgotten summer settles on the back deck.
The railing, concealed with snow, becomes the rotting wood
of an arbor climbing with grapevines and honeysuckle.
Snow-bent sun is the light that arcs off a day bleached

by August and hits the lawn in spaces between
the shimmy of leaves. I am ten years old, hiding
treasures there—rocks, beads, notes to self
that catch me now in the quarter beat of memory.

Soon, we will set up the nursery, swaddle the baby
then watch him grow, leave, the rustle of tissue
as things are wrapped and unwrapped until the paper
is loose as untrammelled snow, the crib casting fence lines
in a field, our footprints obliterated by wind.

NO THOUGHT TO WEATHER

She marries in November, layered in wool and muslin,
no lace, black boots tied to her ankles. Air lattices her lungs
with cold and she coughs out laughter, veils herself in steam
before the horses startle, the sleigh upturns, and the sky bears down,
presses their bodies into snow where arms leave wing prints.

Sixty-five years later, he dies in February, no thought to weather.
Wood heat folds over itself in the egg-domed church and we sing
up to it, wait for it to drop. Barefoot saints stand in drifts of frost
collected at the bottom of windows, their hands raised in small waves
as we follow the priest outside. Wind flattens the snow, pounds
its softness concrete-hard, and she is lowered to kiss his casket.

That afternoon, manufactured heat pumps into the farmhouse.
While we wonder how long she will last, someone lines up
shot glasses on the tray of her wheelchair, and we watch as she tips
thick chilled vodka into her throat, giggles after each swig.
Six years later, she will die in September, late season pollen still
a sticky lace hem on the lake, birds already leaving, calling to each other.

HOW THEY MISS THE FAMOUS STEPS IN ODESSA

Everything prearranged has fallen through.
No smiling young man waits at the airport,
no driver outside, no reservations are on record
as having been made. They find themselves
someone they can trust, a man with cracked teeth
and faintly yellow skin, with eyes so light
that they both hear ice rattling in clear liquid.
He drives them, hour upon grey hour,
to the coast, promise of a seaside paradise,
and they close their eyes, see diamonds of sunlight
cut off water, terraces draped in deep pink flowers.
Instead, in the marble lobby lit by one bare bulb
that swings from somewhere high and dark,
there are litters of kittens mewing, Soviet
orchestral music crackling from a radio, the echo
of Communism cleared out, nothing new rolled in.
The man looks at them, hands twisted into each other.
When they say, *No, not here*, and *Let's go*,
he leads them back to the car, clears the path of wild dogs,
a large stick in his hand arcing through air.

Soon he will introduce them to a woman from Chernobyl
who will bring them a bright bouquet, leave her son
bedridden in the apartment, vomiting into a kitchen bin.
They will think of their own son, crossing the Atlantic
on a sailboat, their daughter, home from India
with wooden beads knotted around her wrist.
A day later, they will drink vodka in the sun
with their new friend, be cajoled to dance in the street,
just steps away from the place where a massacre took place
nearly a hundred years before as the slow burn of revolution
caught on. They will forget to think about history
and fall asleep early, cheeks red, heads cradling dull aches.

BODIES LEFT TO WORDS

This city can be proverbial, a wet blanket,
but my view is expansive. I call him
in another place and watch traffic
clot the spines of bridges
while he replays his day.

His morning began with a deer, found dead
at the side of the road, eaten clean
during the night by the pack of coyotes
that have been skulking around
the cabin, terrifying the cats.

Here, windows smear the white rush
of headlights. There, he pulls
the remains from the ditch,
loads them into a wheelbarrow
and heaves them across the field—

When I got to the grove, ten vultures
were lined up on one branch, staring at me
from some kind of cartoon world.
I did a little dance that scared them,
got back here just in time for your call.

Lights from the street fall into a wineglass
placed on the window sill, the glint
pulls birds from the sky, ready
for bodies left to the woods,
the little dance that follows.

IN SEPTEMBER

For a decade, more, I chose men
to suit one moment, the next, daisy-chained
them together with their similarities:

> Quick hands that pressed knives
> through cloves of garlic. Pick-up trucks.
> Affinity for woodwork. Hobbies—
> botany, astronomy, Russian lit
> —like university catalogues.

I roped sheets around me as I slept,
as though each night I tied myself
to a mast. When we took on water,
stern keeling, I would wait to see who
unhooked the life raft, which one of us
would offer the other the last spot.

My love came in late September
cupped in hands like river currents
—that much, more.

By spring, I kicked off
the sheets. Water licked the edge
of the bed. It tilted then bore our weight—

LOUSY EXPLORERS

The river that once slid through this valley
was damned on its course to the sea, swollen
and put to work. Bloated wood—once banged
together to form a house—still floats up;
rusted nails hold nothing down. Trees shift,
shake their roots free, shoot to split the surface.
Imagine a dislodged pine taking aim
at the underside of sky.

Most things on the ground have long been discovered.
The words *pristine* and *ruin* the double-sided blade
of a paddle that slices us forward, forward.
Rhetoric is slammed down with pints
in the lodge each night, loggers and biologists
both punch-drunk with it. Under water and in the sky
there are things unanswered—fathoms deep, dark matter.
People are working on it as we speak.

There are those of us who try to go to those places
in our minds. Lousy explorers, we make a mess
of things, strip and exploit, squint blindly at stars,
block what should flow. When feeling lucky or foolish,
we let our guns go off, howl at the echo on the lake,
then fancy our largesse, our heavy grace, and sink
deeper, dream pines loosened, quickly rising.

NOTHING TO SEE HERE

There is nothing to see here. Swollen breasts, blue veins
mapping tributaries, planetary belly—all belong
to other women, parks bursting with them.

Your hand cups my stomach, ready, but there is a gap
between palm and abdomen, flattened by lack.
My body, once small, grows smaller.

Slender hips become boyish, tissue looped around bone.
Breasts, once tender as bruised fruit, have lost
their firm centre, fall.

I know. There is no one at fault. But what if I want
that kind of fissure to crack the surface,
want to be torn open, to emerge?

I wait for cells to cluster, drawn together by gravity,
for a big bang, the churn of matter to cool
until it settles. I wait for what will form.

The hot dark centres of stars are hidden from us.
All we see is light punctured into night sky.

LOOK AT US: 2007

I had my doubts, another northern town
built on the felled trees of a dying forest,
satellite dishes spooning the world
into mobile homes that never moved.
I said *yes* and went with him there.

I was over throwing things by then, had learned
that lesson (men don't marry women who toss teacups),
was sensitive to needs—his, mine, how they rubbed
up against each other—attuned to symptoms,
mornings that felt like hangovers without wine.

I wore my hair like I always had, striped it
with more colours, resisted maternity clothes,
yoga pants more practical as I stretched every day
to ease the ache that eddied out
from my back, spined with pain.

I met some great women. Here, look at us:
my selection of hats and love of blue, her self-cut curls
and, for that one, everything had to have an athletic function,
wick things away. See how even in winter I found ways
to show off my belly, that skin-bound moon.

Weekends, we lamented the drugs dropped
and smoked in the last decade, missed them a bit,
while someone's husband lit the barbecue and the guys
got fired up about building boats and shifting
weather patterns, seasons teetering, off-kilter.

Nothing was worse than then,
nothing was better. I had my moods.

PINE CENTRE MALL

Plows push snow to the height
of roof lines, Starbucks blocked
from sight behind mountains that call
for kings of castles, dirty rascals
vying for parking below.

Plastic gift card cutting my palm,
I think of nothing to buy for myself
as valuable as five rolls
of diaper liners, the time I will save
not driving to the mall for them.

Later, the sugar of forced music
sealed away with the swing of the door,
sirens fill the lot. Snow stained
blue and red with lights, cops bend
to collect casings. Things go off

all around us; we don't even know.
Hundred dollar bills were thrown
from car windows, scattered with gunfire.
Shoppers clutch and release their hands.
Possibility of a windfall already gone,

they wait for news teams to arrive.
I am parked beyond circles cast by lights
in the lot, step into dimness, gravel-pocked ice.
I check the back seat before I throw in the bag,
boon of paper, still clean, rolled tight.

FIELD WORK

All night the creek weaves a wet tale between stones,
its low pillow talk. When day splits the sky
along the ridge, we can't hear water

over the clamour of birds, inebriated on early light,
calling to each other, crazy for dawn,
a sleek-winged mate, columns of air.

We unzip the gauze between us and the world—
red sun and fine ash on the tent, signs of fire
somewhere, smoke fingering the spines of mountains.

We flag the forest service road with yellow tape,
GPS unit an unseen string to sky. Things wake up, crash
through the bush. The truck is a bastion of coffee, satellite CBC.

Heat mounts and we shoulder air weighted with smoke
then set up the tent again, hooded by the shade of pines.
Our rest is pockmarked by the crackle of beetles

on their way through bark. I trade sleep to listen
to their dark art while you grind your teeth, dream
of red-tipped wings rising on banks of air.

SHOP NIGHT

Once a week you go into another husband's garage,
band together with home brew, power tools
and instruments, blunt and fine, to build
strip by cedar strip, a boat for us to ride the currents
that cross this place, stitch the map blue.

I get together with another wife. I'm knocked up
and she's sympathetic, both of us tea-tipsy,
my body playing funhouse with hormones. Her kids,
fingers hooked in corners of smiles, careen
toothpaste-mouthed into bedtime.

When they're asleep, the living room is ours to curse
and laugh at how we used to be—chapped-lipped mornings
at bus stops, the sticky feeling of something half-remembered.
You out there in the shop, building things and swilling cheap beer,
makes all the *back then* funnier, all the *right now* lovelier.

You come in with sloppy smiles and flophouse eyes, settle
into couches, mumble about work tomorrow. We couple up
in girl-guy formations, say good night, feel like we're at the centre
of something good, and walk home without talking,
the world cul-de-sacing out around us.

I have little idea what you do on those nights;
you have little idea of my work, the curled slivers of words
pared off around me. We meet in bed, our skin covered
in fine dust, smelling like spent trees, and we hold
our breath, guide each other under.

BOY

Boy, folded like a sail
then snapped open, tears out,
is set afloat. My body a boathouse;
windows broken, curtains bloated
with a lakeful of wind then sucked
back in, empty.

Boy has drunk all he needs
from inside but is still
tethered, uncut, forgets
to cry. Bird calls filter
through screens. Fingers
splayed, he seizes his first air.

Unmoored, he still pulls
blood from me. It surges and pools,
lavic and tidal. My body
unschooled in letting go,
goes overboard. I am strapped
to a plank, borne out

of a room smattered
with sirens' light. God love
the ladies who prick skin, fill me
with radiance, hung from bags,
a slow drip. My body shifting sand,
boy climbs ashore, finds food.

INSOMNIA AND THE IMAGINARY NEW ENGLANDER

Let there be no mobile homes
in the New England of my imagination.
No sleeplessness in my mind's seaside
Maine—belly satisfied with crab,
butter-sated lips, my lover like salt,
and Boston an hour away by train.

In this other present, wind piles up
against the window, leaves trail
sound across the lawn. The cat
balks at the open door—light elongated
across the yard—so we leave him out,
cougar savvy, we hope.

The opposite of amulets, the stories
of how we got here and why, strung together
in the bottom of the night, barbed wire
of thought-spores that track
through sleep then flush out,
a racket in branches.

No entries yet on the list of loving
this place. In my wrong-time wakefulness,
I start a file: wail of train through night,
aspen leaves, field edges fired up
with the turn of trees, poor impersonations
of urbanity that never quite stick.

Then it is almost morning and the flicker's call
is not similar to my slowly turning heart,
the robin is not gathering up its flush feathers
and high-tailing it south to spite me. The sun
spoons the room, thick as maple syrup, and the cat
comes home carrying something in its teeth.

EPIDEMIC

When you said I know you, hello,
and left your hand open on the table,
I fell into it. Imagine my surprise
in your refusal to hold yourself steady—
I was drawn to you, an apple in the palm,
the way things seem simple at first,
like Newton's Law.

Our tactile science—my skin still
August-stained, your smell like October,
leaves underfoot, woodsmoke.
Together we play with gravity, pull ourselves
away from a saturated coast, open
our palms, trace fingers along lines
like magnets that tug us north.

We leave the city on the first of April, fools
for asphalt, for canyons, for following lines
that keep us on the right side of the road.
North through the core of the province,
conversations can't collapse passing time
and the windshield never comes clean.

We take what landscape we can see—
hillsides scorched with the shadows
of ponderosas, horses that kick up clouds
of tumbleweeds, then nothing but forest, forest,
forest, forest. Hours plateau into the drive
and our mouths fill with unsaid words, dry

as pine needles used for tinder. Fire crews wave
us on as roots still smoulder on the roadside.
Later, small blooms of scarlet trees
where the beetles have been. A moose split
down its length, eyes still open. When we see
the Fraser again, we remember water and drink,
give names to kids not yet made.

The day we arrive, they cut down the pines
in the schoolyard behind our rented house.
A month shy of marriage, bodies sore
from the drive, we unload boxes labelled separately.

Men in hard hats and reflective vests
strain the sound of chainsaws through trees.
We unpack, paint every wall as the radio drones
through two weeks' coverage of the Pope's death.

Trees turn red. We hear how plumes of smoke are sent
from the Vatican to mark the departure of His Holiness.
We open boxes, turn things over in our hands,
and smell apples, since eaten, on the newsprint.

In our backyard, twelve pines—green, alive.
Unseen above and around us, airborne
outbreaks of beetles catch thermals.
The trees still living, our hope defiant,
we put our bed near the window to watch
what will fall from the sky—snow, needles, ash.

Five minutes out of the subdivision
and we prepare for encounters—
the sheepish mugs and waddling hindquarters
of bears make our fear quaint
as they scuttle into the bush.

When we run together, we have our voices.
When you run, you carry a large rock
in each hand. When I run alone,
I carry nothing but dumb fear, my heart
a river stone rammed in my throat.

Yellow tape flags the places they will carve
new subdivisions into banks.
Red circles on bark fade to pink,
score decay, mark trees that will be cut,
soft centres split open then chipped.

Bugs carry a plague to which they're oblivious
on their wings. Ford F350s carry women
to Wal-Mart and Costco. A miniature dog barks
soundlessly on the dashboard of a truck.
Flats of bottled water cross parking lots
in the arms of early-season tree planters, still clean.

Up above, somewhere, a helicopter
hews the sky, a hopped-up heartbeat
dopplering away.

June. I can't make it past the foyer,
fall back, boots unlaced. The cat likes me there,
shows me how to roll into the ground,
make it my own. It won't stop
raining. We left rain, we thought we left rain
for this—cul de sacs stamped into the bush,
matchstick pines swaying on the edge of clearings,
slash piles, fire.

Tarp strung, I pound tent pegs and you throw the axe
over your shoulder, lean into the follow-through.
Sun slices around you as though
you are a refraction of waves,
geometry of caught light.

Your back, a template of persistence,
fabric pulled tight with the heave and release
of each muscle as it knots itself to your spine, unfurls.
The pile of split wood grows. I unload food,
check the dark edge for bears.

Nothing is better than cubed meat
on metal plates, red wine straight
from the bottle. Nothing is better than water
off a well-hung tarp, than you over me when the rain
stops and trees bounce off each other in the wind.

By July, we each pocket six weeks,
congratulate ourselves on a marriage
shiny and new, then go in different directions,
hearts palmed like rubbed coins.

This place, the crossroads—
two highways, two rivers, an X
that marks the map's centre, and we keep thinking
of ways to leave, together, apart—

ways to stretch the province, see
what kind of elasticity we hold between us,
if anything will chafe, snap.

When I am away, please, go down to the river,
watch water tear on its folds, roll in on itself.
Cross the bridge, bones cold and bright as chrome
as you collect wind in your jacket.
The other side is where you can lament
the afternoon from a tree trunk strung
like a hammock between cut-bank and sky.
You can attribute living things with your emotions:
when a formation of Bohemian waxwings descends
on a mountain ash, strips it of berries, you can name it *lust*.
When you see something to christen *memory*,
come home, tell the cat about it, call me.

Beetles arrive in our yard while I am gone,
crackle bark as they burrow into sapwood.
Males ride the backs of their mates,
jaws of females agile, insatiable.

You tell me about the base of trees
ringed with wood-dust by nightfall.

When I return the backyard is standing deadwood.
Pairs of pileated woodpeckers, red-crowned and hungry,
bang their heads to slough off bark and gorge
on the arteries of insects branching through trees.

Some nights, we aren't much different, going at each other
for things that might sustain us. Sucking away the rot.

We console ourselves with fires we build
in the backyard. There are pines brittle enough
to break off boughs with our hands. Scabs of sap
blister trees, entry wounds. The cat hunts something in the grass.

Remember when trees tipped, gave in to flames
held underground, roots blazing with the release
of concealed heat. Once fire turned trees black, now
they are red by the mouth of a different kind of death.

Weather once snapped beetles in its jaw
but winter has lost its bite. An old dog
wanders the back forty, comes home
to wait for table scraps.

Next year, the trees are gone. Stumps and wood chips,
firewood bucked into a pyre in the middle of our yard.
The pileateds won't return. Now we see
the helmeted faces of boys who drive ATVs
on the path behind our house, how girls pull
cloaks of hair and cellphones around them
under what trees are still standing.

We are fit for take-off—for leaving
on short notice or for removing
our clothes. We remark how,

with time, flaws in design
are always found. Bark peels
away from trees, trunks smooth

as skin, raw in the places
where the bugs have been.
The fire soaks them with light,

makes shadows of the grooved paths
of beetles. Our hands trace
their conduits, a shifting atlas.

✦

There is no metaphor that connects me
to what is happening to this forest

yet my body branches with foreign life,
mapped by increased blood supply

visible on the surface as I expand,
a colony of rapidly dividing cells

having their way with me—
and whoever has claimed me as theirs.

When the chainsaws begin to bleat
again, we move, choose a house
with no pine in the yard.

We drape coats of green paint
in the nursery then, uncertain,
try another shade of green,

until we decide on yellow.
We let the air out of the house,
doors and windows open to heat

that pushes the city into a cupped palm
of land creased by two rivers,
water swallowing the banks.

Branches shudder with the release
of birds who shake themselves free
from treetops, wing into sky clear of clouds

of beetles who have moved east—
the quake of millions of tiny wings
rising to take on mountains.

Change marks my body, fills me
then leaves me to deflate. It will press
its thumbprint between the eyes
of our baby, claim him.

You and I shuck off the idea of place,
become something larger—
each of us a planet, sun or moon
to each other, circling,

kept on track by an invisible tether
that tells us how far, how long,
how much, when.

NOTES AND ACKNOWLEDGEMENTS

The poem "Lousy Explorers" was inspired by Gwendolyn MacEwen's "Dark Pines Under Water."

"No Thought to Weather" is for the memory of Nelli and Joseph Proch.

"Nothing to See Here" is for Klay Arsenault, who now has everything to see.

"Shop Night" is for Jill and Travis.

Earlier versions of some of these poems appeared in *Event*, *Malahat Review*, *Ontario Review*, *Room* and *The New Quarterly*, and were anthologized in *Rocksalt: An Anthology of Contemporary BC Poets* (Mother Tongue, 2008) and *Verse Map of Vancouver* (Anvil Press, 2009). My sincere thanks to the editors of each. As well, I am grateful to the Canada Council of the Arts for the support of this manuscript in its infancy.

Thank you to my editor, Silas White, for his eye for detail, and to Michelle Winegar and all the people at Nightwood Editions who make it such good harbour from which to launch poetry into the world.

I would like to thank those who read these poems at various stages and whose insights helped them grow to become this book: Aurian Haller, Jason Dewinetz, George Sipos, my fellow Candlefish—Al Rempel, Betsy Trumpener and Gillian Wigmore— and my two constants, Marita Dachsel and Jennica Harper.

As always, I thank my family, including all the extended versions of the Rosnau, Proch, Deans and Seymour clans. And to those for whom the word "thanks" is so small in comparison to what they give me—my son, Jonah, and my husband, Aaron Deans, for inspiration, humour, love, strength, support and everything else.

Author photograph: Bobbi Carpino

laisha rosnau is the author of the best-selling novel *The Sudden Weight of Snow* (McClelland & Stewart) and Acorn-Plantos People's Poetry Prize-winning collection *Notes on Leaving* (Nightwood Editions). Her work has been published in Canada, the US, the UK and Australia, and has appeared in several anthologies including *Breathing Fire 2: Canada's New Poets*, *White Ink: Poems on Mothers and Motherhood* and *Rocksalt: An Anthology of Contemporary BC Poetry*. Born in Montreal and raised in Vernon, BC, Laisha has lived all over British Columbia, most recently in Prince George and Kamloops with her family.